Arduino For Beginners

How to get started with your arduino, including Arduino basics, Arduino tips and tricks, Arduino projects and more!

Introduction

I want to thank you and congratulate you for downloading the book, *"Arduino For Beginners - How to get started with your arduino, including Arduino basics, Arduino tips and tricks, Arduino projects and more!"*.

This book contains proven steps and strategies on how to use Arduino in your tech projects.

Arduino became a popular solution that extends computing and robotics to individuals outside technology field. Hobbyists can do these projects at home while gaining all the advantages this product offers.

This book will teach you all about Arduino and the working components behind its functions. As a beginner, this book teaches you of the concepts, important Arduino parts, basic coding fundamentals and many more.

Towards the end of the book, you'll find several tips and tricks, as well as beginner-level project ideas that will help you master Arduino!

Thanks again for downloading this book. I hope you enjoy it!

Table of Contents

Chapter 1. Arduino Basics: Knowing Arduino

The amazing world computing kept on stirring the minds of individuals interested in this field. They want to get their hands into technological projects using a simple circuit board and program codes. Arduino makes it possible for people outside technology field to create their own devices with specific functions.

In this section, you'll learn about:

- Arduino and its definition

- Where it's used

- Available Arduino types

- Arduino's limitations

Definition

Arduino is a microcontroller developed as an open-source system. It's powered by a chip and composed of different components soldered on the board. It resembles a mini motherboard used in an array of projects.

Arduino is also programmable according to the required functions in a project. Programs will be used to assign certain pins to execute specific tasks. Parts and pins are identified using the labels printed on the board. You'll more about parts and in Chapter 3.

The term "Arduino" is often referred to the actual mini board. However, Arduino board needs to use its software version, also known as Arduino software. It's used for programming commands that indicate the board's purpose or function. More details about Arduino program will be discussed on Chapter 3.

The Advantage of Using Arduino

Many people appreciated this product as it's designed to make robotics and mini computing accessible to regular users. Arduino is marketed for prototyping hobbyists, novice engineers, and those who want to try simple robotics despite the lack of engineering expertise. Everyone who wants to explore robotics and computing can now do projects right at their homes.

Another advantage is its inexpensive price. An Andruino board's price starts at $20 and up depending on the number of installed parts, part types, and slots. The price alone is suitable for beginners who are technically testing Arduino-powered robotics and computing. Hobbyists can complete small projects, which don't usually cost a lot of money, but still offers the features required by developers.

Arduino's open-source and programmable platform brings another benefit. Being an open-source system, Arduino can perform functions required by developers by uploading source codes to get their projects going.

Long-term advantage is using Arduino can help hobbyists build their own boards. Users learn Arduino's architecture by using the board and their functions. Developers can then personalize their future boards according to their projects' complex system.

Finally, Arduino works with different components, allowing designers to be more playful with their project ideas. Projects can be as simple as activating blinking LEDs or blinking or projects that are more mechanical in nature.

What Projects can You Do with Ardruino?

Arduino is a complete device that lets developers do virtually any project. Common and simple projects include developing a small computer for cars, social media "like" counters, MIDI controllers, and a lot more. People who are more ambitious can build small robots, given that the right board is used. Depending on the design and functionalities, a mini robot project may require complicated development.

This board is capable of supporting all these projects through its components, which you'll learn in Chapter 3.

Limitations

Although this system allows hobbyists to do almost everything, Arduino still has its limitations. Its inability to capture and record videos is its main downside. The board's specs are insufficient to support these tasks, which is very different from typical computers and portable devices. These devices are meant for media recording and designed with appropriate components.

However, Arduino is capable of projecting images or graphics through an external display. Unlike capturing videos, projecting won't use as much resources and storage from the board. Also, utilizing an exterior display will handle data conversion to display images or other information. Developers must create a special configuration to make this setup possible.

Available Types

Arduino comes in different models and types. Each model possesses unique features and matches a specific function. As of now, Arduino is distributed in three models. Certain models are available in several variants that cater to special projects' requirements.

Important Things to Remember

Several reminders in using Arduino in your project:

Get the Right Arduino According to Project Requirements

Arduino has different pin numbers and parts depending on the model. Getting the wrong model will result to system incompatibility. Some pins may not work properly when used in other boards.

Another issue is using the wrong board can be confusing for the developer. Project guides specify pin numbers and parts. Being a novice Arduino user, you might get confused when you don't find jumpers, pin numbers, and other vital parts for the project.

Avoid incompatibility issues by reading the guide well. Verify the required board before shopping. Some guides give a link to the indicated Arduino model, which you can click and purchase the recommended board.

Arduino Development is Not Limited to Hardware Knowledge

Using Arduino for a project is not limited to understanding its parts and their respective functions. Your project's success also depends if the code is properly written and successfully loaded to the system. Arduino requires learning the coding process and its fundamental concepts. You must also know how to operate the software and designing codes.

This book will discuss more about coding in Chapter 4.

Chapter 2. Arduino Basics: Arduino Models

Two Arduino models are ideal for beginners' use: Arduino Uno and Arduino Mega. Their features and specifications will be discussed in this section. Other board types will also be mentioned without detailed information since they are meant for advanced Arduino users.

Android Uno

Arduino Uno is the most recommended board for beginners. It's designed for small projects. Similar Uno versions with the same features can be used if preferred.

Uno runs on ATMega328 chip and uses USB, AC/DC adapter or battery as power source. This all-purpose board supports up to 12V power using a wall-wart adapter. Avoid using higher current than 12 volts to avoid risk of overheating. For projects requiring lower current, it has a 5V pin that supports 5 volts of power and other lower voltages. Typical batteries can be utilized as power source, but be wary of the power source draining faster with frequent use.

This model's features include 14 digital input/output (I/O) pins and six analog input pins. Six of the digital I/O pins can be used as PWM. The analog pins' resolution is the maximum of 10 bits , delivering 1024 different reading values.

Model specs include 8-bit CPU, 2KB SRAM, 32 KB flash memory, 1 KB EEPROM, 16MHz clock speed. Its form factor is 2.1 inches by 2.7 inches rectangular board.

Uno's main advantage is having simple circuitry that utilizes small footprint, making it the perfect Arduino for smaller projects. Other pros are accessibility. Uno is widely available and affordable at $30. Users can also find many Uno accessories and shields.

A lot of those who used this board share their projects online. Novice Arduino users have more project options to try with these guides. Guides shared include making a talking clock, thermostat, simple blinking LEDs and many more.

Someone embarking in an Arduino project will find the right projects to begin with through the massive online references available.

As for the disadvantages, this product can run out of pins, particularly if the user won't utilize an external integrated circuit. Another downside is the absence of high memory, which keeps people from using it for special projects.

Arduino Mega 2560

Arduino Mega 2560 is the next recommended Arduino for beginners' projects. It's used for bigger projects that require higher specs. Individuals who are experienced in using this device end up making complicated projects that are guaranteed to work with Mega. Beginners can also try using this device if they aim for complex projects that their current skills can accomplish.

Mega is almost the same as Uno, except that it has more features, especially I/O pins. It has 70 I/O pins that let users plug more components. Out of 70 pins, 54 of them are digital I/O pins and the remaining are analog pins. Specs include 8KB SRAM, 256KB flash memory, and 4KB EEPROM. Due to its massive features, this Arduino can hold programs four times larger than Uno's supported capacity.

Using this device has a lot of advantages. Aside from massive number of I/O pins, it also comes in two variations that meet developers' requirements further. The first variation is *Due* that has 32-bit ARM, which is faster and offers more resources to support advanced projects. Nevertheless, it only runs at 3.3V power.

Another variation is ADK, which is designed for Android phones. This is a common choice for individuals wanting to explore mobile device computing.

Other advantages are the generous memory capacity and storage space for coding and running programs. It can run massive projects without using external integrated circuits and as long as projects carefully thought out. Just like with Uno, individuals using Mega will find a lot of projects online provided by individuals who have been using the device for a long time.

Although its features are regarded ideal for a lot of beginners dreaming of larger projects, it also has its disadvantages like the need for modifying codes. Guides shared for this Arduino often requires people to change codes slightly depending on the pin numbers. Another disadvantage is it's more expensive than Arduino Uno, which may not be as practical for beginners. Although it's only twice as much in terms of price, it may not be recommended due to chances of damaging the board while in the middle of setting up the project.

Its availability in stores as well as accessories needed to execute the project with it may also be challenging. It's not as widely available as Uno. Users may need to look for Mega in in overseas stores. As for accessories, it doesn't have as many shields available in stores. You'll find out more about shields in the next section.

Other Arduino Models

Other Arduino models are available for higher end projects. These models won't be discussed in detail since they are not recommended for beginners.

- *Arduino Pro.* Arduino Pro is for more advanced and professional developers. It has similarities with Uno in terms of power capacity and the lack of header pins. Connections must be soldered onto the board for them to function. Hence, using Pro requires expert or professional handling. It's also ideal for projects that must be permanently embedded together. Pro variations include Mini, Fio and Micro.

- *LilyPad.* LilyPad differs from all discussed Arduino types due to shape. Instead of having rectangular form factors, this device comes in round shape with flower-like pattern. This device is ideal for constructing wearable systems and e-textiles. It's washable and those who have used it claimed that using a mild soap shouldn't be a problem in washing the device.

Chapter 3. Arduino Basics: A Look at the Hardware

The main board is serves as the core of an Arduino's project. Its parts convert data to execute require functions. This chapter teaches you about:

- Arduino parts and their respective labels.

- Tools used for setting up the project.

- Basic procedures beginners must know.

Parts

Arduino is comparable to a regular computer motherboard with its parts working together in distributing signals from input to output channels, power distribution, and execute coded functions. Parts placements or their locations within the board are different depending on the models. As a beginner, you must learn some basic parts that are crucial for your project.

Processor or Integrated Circuit

Just like computers, a processor serves as the center of entire board operation. Due to the Arduino's small form factor, its processor also comes small in size with varying capacities depending on the board model.

An Integrated Circuit (IC) can be long or square black plate with metal legs often placed above the Analog pins and Power pins section. It acts as Arduino's main processing unit or brain. Different IC types are compatible for specific project, which stresses the importance of verifying required Arduino before purchasing.

Power Supply

A power supply is the electricity gateway used for activating the entire board. The electricity will flow through embedded circuits towards the connected parts. Power transmitted will activate the parts to do their tasks like receiving and analyzing signals then process conversion. To ensure proper board function, it should have smooth power flow that keeps the system activated.

Power supply sources can be placed through USB port or a barrel jack. USB connection, just like in flash drives, distributes electricity throughout the board.

The USB port's size in Arduino is the same as those installed in computers. The size is enough to fit a typical USB cable. However, not all boards have USB ports, which can be a problem if you prefer using USB connection as power gateway. Check the power supply source first online before purchasing an Arduino board.

USB port's function is not limited to power distribution. It's also used for loading codes to the board. You'll write the code on your computer then load it to the board through USB just like the usual file transfer process.

Another power supply source is the barrel jack or power jack. A power jack is a typical external power source. It got its name due to its barrel-like shape embedded on an exposed board. It looks like a typical power jack for mobile devices and works with an adapter. The barrel jack is installed on a board using three metal prongs that conduct electricity.

Power Supply Jumpers

Power supply jumpers let you toggle or choose between two power supplies. Activate your preferred power source using the jumper and it will temporarily deactivate other power source. For example, your board can get power through USB connection and an adapter through the power jack. But for now, you prefer getting power through USB connection. Set the jumper to USB and the board will only receive power from USB connection. Therefore, the system won't power up upon plugging an adapter into the jack. If you prefer otherwise, set the jumper to power jack and the system will activate once an adapter is used.

The power jumper looks like a switch placed in between labels "USB and EXT". It's located in between the USB port and the power jack or power regulator.

Keep in mind that a jumper is not always labeled. The board's diagram makes it easy for advanced Arduino users to spot the jumper. Several board models may not have this option. Verify this information by visiting the board's website or downloading its data sheet.

Analog Pins

Analog pins are used for transferring data or signals from an analog sensor. You'll locate a group of analog pins by looking for the label "Analog In," which stands for

"Analog Input". The analog signal or data will then be converted to digital data shown on displays like LCD displays or external graphics output. An Arduino can have more than one pin depending on the model. The set of analog pins are often located at the lower right corner, if you're looking at the board with the power jack on the lower left side.

Digital Pins

Located at the topmost side of the board are the digital pins, which are used for input/output devices. It can be used for reading digital signals or data then interpreting it to digital output. A common example is digital input from pushing a button which then translates to output like lighting a LED bulb. Just like analog input, a board can have several digital pins based on the model.

Reset Button

Reset Button functions similarly as gaming consoles' reset buttons. When pushed, it will ground and restart Arduino's code. This component is helpful for people using non-repetitive codes. It looks like a typical button with "Reset" label. The button's placement varies on the Arduino model.

Power Pins

The power pins refer to the pins connected for power distribution. It is a group of pins working for this function. This group is often found beside the analog pins group and labeled "Power". Pins under this group are:

- **Ground** (GRN). Ground serves as a reference point in connecting components with varying voltage capacities. It sets a common ground that prevents high voltage current from flowing thru low voltage connections. Ground connections let you install a 12V part to a 5V Arduino. The number of ground connections varies on model. Ground pins are often found with analog and digital pin groups.

- **Pulse-Width Modulation (PWM)**. Pulse-width modulation is another term referring to a digital signal type. It allows Arduino to carry out sophisticated circuitry control like fading LED light through analog output simulation.

- **Analog Reference (AREF)**. Users may or may not use this pin depending on the project. Oftentimes, it sets analog input pins' upper limits, usually from zero to 5V.

- **IOREF**. This pin indicates the required voltage to operate the microcontroller. IOREF values are different across Arduino models. For example, Arduino UNO supplies 5V to IOREF pin while Duo supplies 3V.

LED indicator

An Arduino has one LED light serving as power indicator. It lights up when the board is connected to a power source. An activated LED means power is distributed properly throughout the board. Failing to light up indicates probable circuitry issues that affect power distribution or power source problems.

Voltage Regulator

The voltage regulator is a component that stabilizes power's voltage as it flows within the board. However, it can't tolerate extremely high voltage power sources. Experts recommend not to plug Arduinos to a power source with over 20 volts.

This component is located the barrel jack and USB port and characterized by a rectangular black panel with three protruding legs.

Components

An Arduino board is only a single part of a project. Other components will be installed together with it to ensure the project will function as expected. Aside from Arduino PCB, the following components must be verified on guides and purchased for the project:

Shields

Shields are components placed on top of the main Arduino board to extend its capabilities. These components can be purchased together with Arduino PCB at the same shop. Although it may look like a cover for Arduino, it has similar design with the main PCB, which makes it work like a feature extender.

Different types of shields are available that will work well depending on the project. Examples of commonly used shields are the following:

- **Xbee.** Xbee is a shield that serves as wireless communication gateway in between Arduino boards up to 100 feet in distance when indoors. The distance capacity can increase by up to 300 feet when used in an outdoor space. It needs the Maxtream Xbee Zibgee module as the main component to function as a wireless connection device.

- **Motor Control.** This module lets users control and manipulates DC motors and reading their encoders.

- **Custom Shields.** Some developers think that customizing their own shields is the best solution for their projects. They want to customize the function they'll get in using the additional device. Luckily, developers can create their own shields by following guides online. Beginners are recommended to use specific guides for custom shields. Be reminded, however, that customizing another PCB may require expertise depending on the series complexity.

Wire

Wires are the actual connectors that aid electricity flow or data transfer. They are the basic components used in developing technical systems. Developers may refer to any component or device that conducts electricity in between other Arduino devices as wire. There are two types of wire used with Arduino: the physical wire and wire gauges.

The physical wire comes in solid or stranded wire categories. These wire categories depend on the wire flexibility called for by a project. A solid wire is ideal for a project that doesn't need it to bend or flex. Placing at least one solid wire can simplify the work required for Arduino projects. A good example of such project is in buildings - the wire won't bend and the system will only use a single connection instead of several stranded wires, which have the tendency to bend excessively and result to problematic handling.

Stranded wire is the most flexible wire often used as appliances cords or cables for audio and video output.

Wire gauges are utilized with breadboards. It supports the installation of 22 gauge wires, but it can also handle a gauge or two if needed. It can have headers like female headers, which can't be used for wire insertion, but will work effectively in prototyping projects. Many novice developers may have a hard time choosing between 20 and 22 wire gauges. The 20-gauge wire may be slightly dependable than 22 gauge ones, but will certainly work.

Breadboard

Breadboard refers to the component utilized for circuit construction and testing. It looks like a small white board with many square holes in it. A breadboard is usually incorporated in a prototyping project. There are different types of breadboard that meet specific project demands. A common type is a solderless breadboard. Wires are inserted through the breadboard holes then connect on the metal strips below. Utilizing a breadboard keeps users from soldering wires and connectors and still retains them in place.

Capacitor

This small component retains and releases electrical charge in a circuit connection. It usually has two charging plates and an additional material that controls electricity discharge. They come in different types, but indicated on Arduino's product descriptions for buyers' reference.

They can be produced with different features, with some sold mainly for storage due to their sizes. Store charge capacity is represented in Farads (F).

Resistor

A resistor resists electricity flow, which guarantees smooth electricity flow within the system. It's a must-have component on PCBs for protection in instances of power fluctuation, which affects the entire project. Their capacities are measured in Ohms (R) or (Ω).

Inductor

An inductor is a solution that keeps electrical energy within a magnetic field. It's a wire coil that produces a magnetic field whenever current is distributed throughout the board. Energy increase during distribution promotes higher energy stored in the field. When it decreased, energy is converted and released as electrical power. Induction capacity is measured in Henrys (H).

Diode

A diode is a device that permits one-way or unidirectional electricity flow. Several types of diode types are available with specific functions. The most common is light emitting diode (LED) and photo diode that detects light.

LED

As a diode, LED can produce a specific wavelength of light upon receiving specific electricity voltage or also called the forward voltage. As an example, a bright LED means it receives high voltage electricity and dimmer when lower voltage circulates in the PCB.

Since this device doesn't have any limiting feature, it receives the full voltage and causes overheating. Overheating causes LED to be burned out easily. A burned out LED will still activate with decreased brightness unlike its original wavelength.

Pushbutton

A pushbutton is a device that controls electricity flow in a circuit. It can either complete or stop electricity flow with a trigger on the button. There are many types of pushbuttons compatible with specific projects and come with special configurations. A favorite among developers is the momentary switch.

Transistor

A transistor is a device that permits current flow between two points by utilizing a third component. Current flow happens if the third point of contact is present or not. It comes with three leads and available in two types.

Relay

Relay depends on mechanical movement to complete a connection between two points. It comes with a special type of contact switch utilizing solenoid as one of its components. It can switch mechanisms to interchange low DC current with larger AC currents.

Included Procedures

Several procedures are required to bring a board together. Circuits must be connected by plugging wires and setting a ground to produce a good point of reference for electrical current.

Perhaps the most challenging part of using this board is soldering. Soldering is the process of connecting two conductors together by melting a lead on the connection then letting it cool down. Once cooled, the lead becomes hard enough to keep the wires together in place.

Chapter 4. Arduino Basics: A Look at the Software

Studying Arduino software is the next lesson to study after learning the hardware. Learning about the software is as important as complex coding is needed to generate desired results in building a project. Guides can help you get familiarized with the software.

In this section, you'll learn about:

- Arduino software in general.

- Software installation procedures.

- Connecting the hardware with the software.

- Loading Codes to Arduino.

- Coding fundamentals.

Getting to Know Arduino Software

Arduino software is the program used for coding and transferring codes to the hardware. Different types of Arduino software are available and compatible with major operating systems. The latest version is Arduino 1.6.4., an opensource program with easy to use interface once installed, with versions compatible with Windows, Mac and Linux. Although installation procedures across operating system types are different, users must follow a standard rule in uploading the programmed code.

The Installation Process

The general rule is installing the Arduino software first before using the Arduino PCB. Installation procedures are as follows:

1. Look and select Arduino board from online shops. Aside from the board, you must also get a USB cable to connect the board to the computer.

Different Arduino models come with their compatible USB cables. Be mindful of the cable required by reading the model's description.

2. Download the program compatible with your computer's operating system. The program is available at Arduino's website, with the standard Arduino software listed first being the most recommended platform to use. Other program options are available, but they may require special installation procedures. Furthermore, using another program tends to void your Arduino's warranty. Verify these procedures first and see the instance when your product's warranty may be voided.

3. Extract and install the downloaded program.

4. Plug the board to the computer using the USB cable after installation. Some Arduinos like Uno and Mega obtain power through USB connection. These boards should power up immediately once plugged to a computer.

   Some models supporting external and USB power sources should be configured properly to receive electricity through USB cable. A good example is Diecimila, which supports two types of electricity sources. Set the jumper, the switch-like device discussed in the previous chapter, to USB for now as its power source. Once configured, plug the board to the computer. Its LED will light up once electricity flows throughout the circuitry.

5. Install Arduino drivers. Just like external devices, your computer's operating system must install Arduino's driver first before it can receive codes. The board works like a plug and play device. The operating system will detect the new device once plugged in and install its drivers. However, this procedure may fail since you need to configure the driver manually.

   Once drivers failed to install, open Device Manager and look at Ports (COM & LPT). Your Arduino should be listed under this group as "Arduino (Model) (COMxx)". If not listed, search under "Other Devices" and look for "Unknown Device". It means your computer detected the newly plugged device, but it can't identify the new component correctly due to the lack of pre-installed drivers. Right click or double click on the Arduino model and look for "Update Driver Software" option. You'll be directed to another dialog box. Choose "Browse my computer for driver software". Locate the Arduino installer and look for the "Drivers" folder that comes with it. Select "Arduino.inf" to install.

There instances, however, when "Arduino.inf" is missing. Using older IDE versions like 1.0.3. and other earlier versions often cause this issue. In this scenario, look for the driver that has the Arduino's model name in it. For instance, if you're using Arduino Uno, look for the file "Arduino UNO.inf". Selecting the file will cause the operating system to install the file and it's ready to go.

Differences in operating system may also affect the software installation process. Installation is an instant process in newer operating systems like Windows 7 or Vista. Installation in Windows XP can be slightly complicated with its older interface developed earlier by Microsoft.

When the device is plugged in, it should display the "Add New Hardware" dialog box that installs the Arduino software. Don't let the operating system look for drivers in Windows Update. Choose "Install from a list or specified location (Advanced)". Click next and you'll be directed to the next prompts. Tick the box for "Search for the best driver in these locations" and uncheck "Search removable media". Tick "Include this location in the search" and look for the drivers/FTDI USB Drivers directory.

Since it's possible that available drivers are outdated, download newer driver versions by visiting FTDI website. Click next and the system should start searching for the new device. It will report about finding a "USB Serial Converter". Click it and complete the installation process. Once done, the newly installed hardware should be found under Ports (COM & LPT).

6. Open Arduino software to see sample codes. It comes with pre-set codes that can be used as reference for beginners. Load the blink example in the program by clicking File > Examples > Basics > Blink. You will see a list of

code together with the description or function of what the code should do on the product. For example, the code indicates that this command will turn a LED on and off with a duration of a second each run repeatedly.

7. Load example codes to Arduino. Select the board type under Tools > Board. Clicking on the Arduino model will place a check on the selected option. Next, choose the port allotted for the device. Usually, the Arduino board ports are COM3 or higher. The first two ports, COM1 and COM2, are usually designated for hardware serial ports. If you're unsure of the right port, open the menu first the look for the available ports. List them down if needed. Disconnect your board then re-open the menu. The missing port should be the one assigned for your Arduino. Reconnect it and select to upload the code.

   After selecting the port, click Upload to load the programmed code. You'll know that codes are being processed and uploaded light flashes on the board. The computer will display a dialog box saying "Done uploading," which means the code has been successfully uploaded.

8. Observe the effects. Wait for several seconds after completing the upload and you'll see the board's LED lights blinking.

Coding Fundamentals

Although you're a beginner, you must know more about coding fundamentals or the basic terms you will often see in writing codes. Being knowledgeable of the terms will help you code faster in the long run.

Variables

Variables refer to the container used for keeping the data. It declares a data's value, indicates its name, and highlights the function type expected. The code syntax is:

Type Variable = Value

So, if you have pin number 14 and int as a type, you can code it as:

int pin = 14

This value will be applied throughout the new codes placed in the Arduino program. Typing the value frequently is unnecessary. The system will automatically detect the value and function according to the set variable. For example, in this code:

pinMode(pin, OUTPUT)

Since you've declared the value of pin in "int pin=14" code as 14, the system will use the same pin value all throughout the code.

The coding process will make you think if declaring value through variable is necessary. Why not just type the value over and over again than write complex and confusing code? The main advantage is you will only declare the value once and it will be used repeatedly in the code. No need to type the value manually because the software will automatically detect it.

Declaring a variable's value can be done right at the beginning of the code to declare the global value. When you declare a global value, the software should use the assigned value throughout the code. For example,

```
int pin = 14

void setup()

{

pinMode(pin, OUTPUT);

}

void loop()

{

digitalWrite(pin, High)

}
```

This code has two functions, which you'll learn more in the next section. Notice that the pin value assignment is placed at the top, which means the value will be global or used throughout the entire code.

Changing the pin's value is also possible with a simple command. Nevertheless, you must be careful in declaring the value because they may or may not change the value then result to an error message. An example of coding to change the value is this code:

```
int pin = 14

void setup()

{

 pin = 15

 pinMode(pin, OUTPUT);

}

void loop()

{

 digitalWrite(pin, High)

}
```

The value of pin in digitalWrite() part will also change as it's assigned on top of the code as a global value.

If you want to change a pin's value in a certain function, you can type it in a manner where the value is only interpreted as a part of a specific function. For example:

```
void setup()

{

 int pin = 15;

 pinMode(pin, OUTPUT);

 digitalWrite(pin, High);

}
```

In this case, the new value of 15, will only be used in this function.

There are instances when you may experience error message after declaring a value. Example:

void setup()

{

int pin = 15;

pinMode(pin, OUTPUT);

digitalWrite(pin, High);

}

void loop()

{

digitalWrite(pin, LOW);

}

You've declared the pin value, but the value for *digitalWrite* under *loop()* won't read and use 15. Reason being is the pin value assigned is not within the function's scope. Assigned value is for *setup()*, but not for *loop()*. Regardless of where the code is placed, the system won't be able to recognize the code you just placed.

Function

A function refers to the line of code used to define a task. When loaded, a function will execute the task as described in the code. Programmers can even use a single function and use it several times if desired.

Since a function serves an indicator, new Arduino users would ask if placing the code in function segments is still necessary. Placing a full code in segmented functions has its benefits, with organization as the main reason. It helps developers organize their codes. Functions' keywords indicate developers about what they can do once loaded to a board.

Another advantage of segmentation is it aids developers to spot their needed codes immediately. Arduino developers must use some functions multiple times. Referring to the previously used codes will be less demanding than typing them again, saving developers more time in creating their programs.

Dissecting a Function

In Arduino, a function needs to have a *setup()* and *loop()*. They are the main function codes that beginner must learn. On the other hand, the system will know that the new code is outside through brackets, which are required coding symbols.

Look at the following code to dissect the parts of a function:

int myMultiplyFunction(int x, int y) {

int result;

result = x * y

return result;

}

- **Function name.** A function name refers to the task to be done in the code. In creating a simple calculation code, it will be the variable to be displayed or what the function is for. For instance, the function name in the aforementioned code is *myMultiplyFunction*

- **Parameters.** Parameters refer to the value a function inherited. In this case, the parameters are *int x* and *int y*.

- **Return Statement.** A return statement refers to the type of data that matches the declaration. Return statement is easy to spot in this code because it has the word "return".

- **Datatype of returned data.** This is the returned value after the code has been activated. When a value returned, it will show *int*, which is found in the first part of the code. In case there's no value was returned after loading a code, then the datatype will be *void*.

Now that you know what these codes stand for, you will learn about sample projects that you can do on your own. For now, coding won't discussed in depth with you being a beginner Coding won't be describe in detail at this point with you being a beginner. However, you'll see more codes upon doing some projects.

Chapter 5. Troubleshooting and Fixing Arduino Issues

There are instances when your Arduino program or hardware won't function properly. The problem can be caused by software or hardware issues like incompatibility. This section is dedicated to troubleshooting and solving Arduino problems on software and hardware level.

Can't Load Programs on Arduino

Loading program should be easy given that you have the right program and the right board. There are several reasons why you can't load codes into the system.

The problem can range from missing the right drivers, board, or using the wrong port in the software. In terms of hardware problems, the problem can be caused by problematic physical connection or the device firmware.

Solution: Verify Board Model and Configured Model

The first solution is double-checking the Arduino model configured on the program. Some users tend to select the wrong type of board on the program. Verify the model used then access Tools > Board menu on Arduino software. Once you have selected the right board type, you can reload the code and see if it will be loaded.

Another thing to check is the type of microcontroller on the board. For example, several Arduino boards have ATmega 160 microcontroller, particularly the older boards. The newer ones have ATmega328. If you're confused as to what to choose, you can look at the microcontroller on the board and select it on the device.

Driver problem is also a common problem why the system won't load the code. See if the driver is installed by checking Tools > Serial Port. Be sure that the board is connected to the computer in verifying this information.

Another place to check is the device manager in your computer. Look if there are some items that are marked yellow or unidentified in the device. If you don't know some drivers that probably causing the problem, the marked driver should be the one belonging to Arduino board. You may need to reinstall or update the driver by accessing its properties and installing the driver. You can review the process of installing drivers through the previous chapter.

Solution: Ensure a Functioning Arduino

Your computer may not detect the device if it doesn't have any power. Verify if the board itself is receiving electricity by looking at its LED. If it's not working, then the system is probably not getting any electricity. Check the power supply source and see if it's working.

If you have a board with dual power option, see if the jumper is set to receive electricity from your desired source. For instance, if you're using USB to power your board, look if the jumper is directed towards the USB side, which means the system should get power from this source. If not, disconnect the device first, set the jumper to the power source, and plug it again. Check if the LED indicator turns on to see if it will start working.

Solution: Reset the Device

An Arduino board has a reset device, which will be useful in loading problems while transferring codes. Reset the board using the reset button. Press and reset it for several seconds. After the waiting time, reload the program and see if it's working.

Solution: Diagnose USB Connection Problem

Most of the time, the hardware connection itself is causing the inconsistency. Code transfer won't be completed if the data pathway itself is busted. Solve this problem by changing your USB cable. There are several ways in diagnosing whether the cable is the problem. If you plug the board to your computer and it doesn't seem to detect it, try connecting using a different cable. Through the Arduino program, check if the serial port that should be assigned on your board is present or not.

Arduino Software is Not Working

Programs tend to not work as expected. An Arduino software that doesn't load properly is probably installed using a wrong or outdated program version than what the operating system requires. Usually, software incompatibility issues should render you unable to install the program to your computer. In this case, uninstall the program, download the newer version of the compatible installer then reinstall.

Another reason is the probability is you're using a third party Arduino program. Third party Arduino programs should work properly as promoted by Arduino developers. Uninstall your current program and download a new installer from the third party developer's official website. Don't download a file from other sources. Extract the file and install.

If the aforementioned solution failed, download the actual Arduino program. Install then see if the program will load.

Arduino Software is Freezing and Crashing

A freezing Arduino software is caused by program inconsistency. The conflicting program can be a process installed with a computer peripheral, driver or other files. Diagnose probable conflicting program using MSConfig. Load this utility and disable Startup programs and services. Restart your computer and load Arduino software. If Arduino program loaded flawlessly, there's a chance that one of your startup program is causing the issue. Try and test each program and service to identify the cause. Remember the result because you will need to end the process first before loading Arduino software to prevent lagging.

In some cases, the program is running slowly although it doesn't freeze or crash. This is also probably caused by some devices installed in your computer. A typical culprit is an installed of the COM port meddling with the loading process. Use MSConfig again to disable and diagnose program causes. Turn off your computer then unplug all the other devices in your computer. Turn the computer on then plug the device. Load the program and see if it's responding properly.

Chapter 6. Additional Tips and Tricks

Additional tips and tricks in using Arduino are always helpful for beginners. Take note of the following ideas to maximize your experience in using this PCB:

Don't Throw Damaged Arduino

The chances of damaging an Arduino PCB q43 are high for beginners. Don't worry because it happens as part of the learning process.

In case you damage a board, don't throw it away. You can still use it in getting familiarized with its parts. Dismantle its parts if you want to have an idea how each piece is installed. Doing so will be helpful once you're ready to create your custom board.

Save RAM through Coding

Writing a code saves the data in two locations: in the RAM and program memory. Program memory saves all the information while RAM deletes them once power supply in the board is interrupted. Activating the board requires RAM to copy the usual strings from the program memory. Therefore, you're using more resources that may slow down your project.

A good example of code that saves memory is Serial.println(F("Text to insert")); instead of writing it as Serial.println("Text to insert"). The former will draw out the text from the program memory via temporary buffer. No need for RAM to copy and load the data, which saves memory resources.

Take Note of Extra or Missing Code Characters

Make sure that the code you type doesn't have extra character. An additional character will keep the system from generating desired functions or results. Double check the code and remove extra characters.

The same goes for missing characters. Be sure to place semicolon on codes because it's a mandatory symbol.

Take Advantage of *Serial.list()* Command

Arduino program must read the board from the right port. You will know the available ports in your computer by typing *Serial.list()*. This command will list down all available ports for your board.

Add Notes on the Codes if Necessary

Writing notes on your codes is a good practice. You'll remember what the code is for or the result it should generate. Add a note beside a code line by setting a space then two slashes (//) then type your notes. For example:

```
int pin = 14

void setup()

{

pin = 15

pinMode(pin, OUTPUT); // Note 1 here.

}

void loop()

{

digitalWrite(pin, High) // Note 2 here.

}
```

The slashes are an indicator that the next characters are not part of the code. The system won't interpret the characters and meddle with the results.

Take Precautionary Measures before Assembling

Although you're doing a simply project, Arduino installation requires safe handling. Soldering can burn and wound your fingers or hands. A drop of melted lead can also be painful on your skin. Follow soldering and building guides accordingly to keep you from accidents.

Start with the Following Projects

Start playing with Arduino hardware and software by doing the following simple projects. Follow the links to see the procedures and detailed list of needed parts:

- An e-dice using Arduino Uno
- A basic stopwatch
- A bar graph display
- A garage door opener
- An Arduino Drone (Italian)
- Thermostat

Conclusion

Thank you again for downloading this book!

I hope this book was able to help you to be familiarized with Arduino and its advantages to non-technology experts and hobbyists who want to build their own tech systems at home.

The next step is to do some recommended projects and learn proper handling and installation process for Arduino. Hone your skills and challenge yourself to bigger projects using Arduinos with higher specs.

Finally, if you enjoyed this book, then I'd like to ask you for a favor, would you be kind enough to leave a review for this book on Amazon? It'd be greatly appreciated!

Click here to leave a review for this book on Amazon!

Thank you and good luck!

Preview Of 'Insert Book Title Here'

This section is designed to provide the reader a preview of one of your other books. Simply copy and paste a chapter of another book that you have available on Kindle and link to it below.

Click here to check out the rest of (insert book name here) on Amazon.

Or go to: **http://www.mybitlylink.com** (insert shortened bit.ly link)

Made in the USA
Las Vegas, NV
16 February 2025

18225316R00022